FROM THE HANDS OF A CHILD

Special Seasonal Art Activities for Primary Children

by Anthony Flores

Fearon Teacher Aids
A Division of Frank Schaffer Publications, Inc.

Contents

This Fearon Teacher Aids product was formerly manufactured and distributed by American Teaching Aids. Inc., a subsidiary of Silver Burdett Ginn, and is now manufactured and distributed by Frank Schaffer Publications, Inc. FEARON, FEARON TEACHER AIDS and the FEARON balloon logo are marks used under license from Simon & Schuster, Inc.

© Fearon Teacher Aids
A Division of Frank Schaffer Publications, Inc.
23740 Hawthorne Boulevard
Torrance, CA 90505-5927

ISBN 0-8224-3167-X

Printed in the United States of America

Illustrator: Pat Gavett

Introduction

From the Hands of a Child provides you with art lessons that are unique for each child. As in many art activity books, the lessons are seasonal by month. Yet each of these activities is special because it incorporates the hand tracings of each individual child. Parents and children will want to date and save these creations.

Each lesson includes teacher's notes and a reproducible pattern page. The activity directions are printed on the pattern page and are an excellent resource for practice in reading and reinforcing skills in following directions. With these art projects, children will practice cutting various shapes, arranging paper pieces to create pictures, and pasting pieces neatly. The projects also offer practice with color and shape recognition and with spatial awareness.

The color combinations indicated are not required. You may want to allow children to choose other colors than those listed in the lessons. The necessary materials for each art project are listed in the teacher's notes, but the paper sizes are approximate. You may want to encourage the children to add other cut-paper or felt-marker decorations to their projects.

General Directions for All Projects

Duplicate the pattern pages on heavy paper, which is easier for young children to cut. Provide box lids so that each student may keep his or her pattern pieces at hand during the art lesson. (Small pattern pieces are apt to fly off the desk and get lost.)

Distribute the required materials. Ask the students to read the directions on the pattern page with you. Explain the symbols in the directions: ✐ means to draw, trace, or write; ✄ means to cut; and ⬓ means to paste. Young children or developmentally disadvantaged children who cannot read may be able to complete the projects independently, using the direction symbols, the pictures of the pattern pieces, and the sample of the completed project.

Demonstrate the best ways of tracing the children's hands. (Sometimes an activity may call for a spread-out hand; sometimes for a fairly closed hand.) Show the students how to fold construction paper in half and how to place patterns on the folds efficiently. With primary students, make sure they understand the directions thoroughly before they proceed with the lesson. Capable second- or third-graders, however, may be able to complete some of these art projects independently without initial guidance.

September

Apple Time

Materials for each child:
- red, green, and brown construction paper
- pattern page
- scissors and paste

This project helps provide practice with cutting large, simple shapes, arranging them to match a pattern, and recognizing color words and their colors.

All About Apples

Materials for each child:
- blue, brown, and lime green construction paper
- pattern page
- scissors and paste

This activity may require two class periods to complete. Students may need to prepare a draft story during the first session on a plain sheet of paper. Younger children may dictate a story to you or to a volunteer. Apple wedges make a good snack before the draft story writing session.

To make an attractive bulletin board display, pin each completed project on a board covered with background paper, and cut out letters to make a display heading **All About Apples.** Stress size discrimination between big and small apples.

Back to School

Materials for each child:
- green, red, blue, and brown construction paper
- pattern page
- scissors and paste

This project provides children with practice in recognizing several shapes, color words and their colors, and reproducing a set pattern. You may want to allow them to arrange the pieces in a different way than shown. Remind children to trace one right hand and one left hand. Discuss how the right and left hands are the same and how they are different (symmetry).

Falling Leaves

Materials for each child:
- brown, green, orange, and blue construction paper
- pattern page
- scissors and paste

The children should spread their fingers wide before tracing their hands to create branches of the tree. Discuss autumn and how some trees lose their leaves during this season. Children may enjoy pasting a few real leaves on their projects. These may be collected during a neighborhood walk. Be sure the children understand that they must trace and cut out five copies of the leaf pattern.

Apple Time _____

1.  around 1 ✋ on green paper.
2. ✂ it out.
3. ✂ out the 🍎 below.
4. ✏ the 🍎 on red paper.
5. ✂ it out.
6. ✏ the 🌿 on green paper.
7. ✂ it out.
8. 🖌 the 🍎 🌿 ✋ on brown paper.
9. ✏ your name on the brown paper.

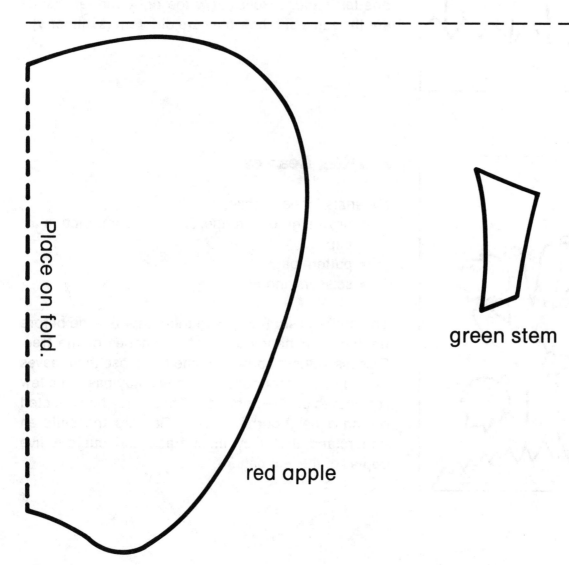

Place on fold.

red apple

green stem

4

All About Apples

1. ✏️ around 2 🖐️ 🖐️ on brown paper.

2. ✂️ them out.

3. ✂️ out the 🌰🌰 below.

4. ✏️ the 🌰🌰 on the green papers. 📄

5. ✂️ them out.

6. ✏️ a story on the big 🍎.

7. 🖌️ the 🍎🍎🖐️🖐️ on blue paper.

8. ✏️ your name on the blue paper.

Jane

I like apples. Apples taste sweet. They grow on trees.

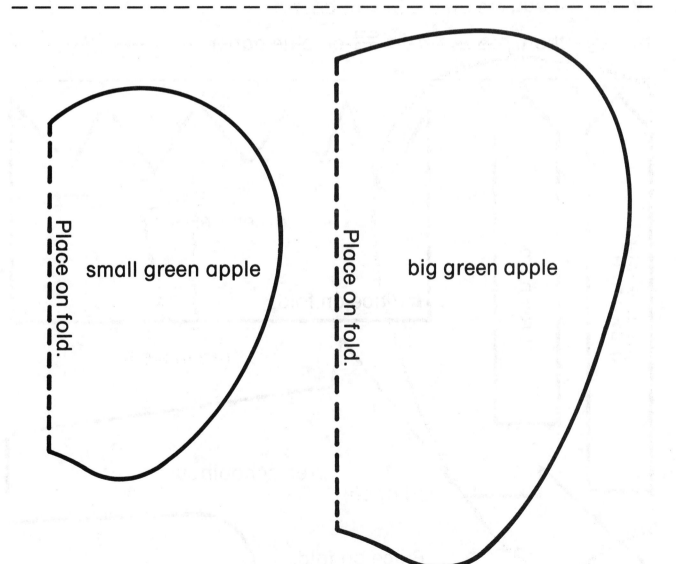

small green apple

Place on fold.

big green apple

Place on fold.

Back to School

1. ✏️ around 2 🖐️ 🖐️ on green paper.
2. ✂️ them out.
3. ✂️ out the ✏️ ☰ 〰️ below.
4. ✏️ the ✏️ on red paper. 📖
5. ✂️ it out.
6. ✏️ the ☰ on brown paper.
7. ✂️ them out.
8. ✏️ the 〰️ on green paper. 📖
9. ✂️ it out.
10. 🖌️ the 🏠 〰️ 🖐️ 🖐️ ☰ on blue paper.

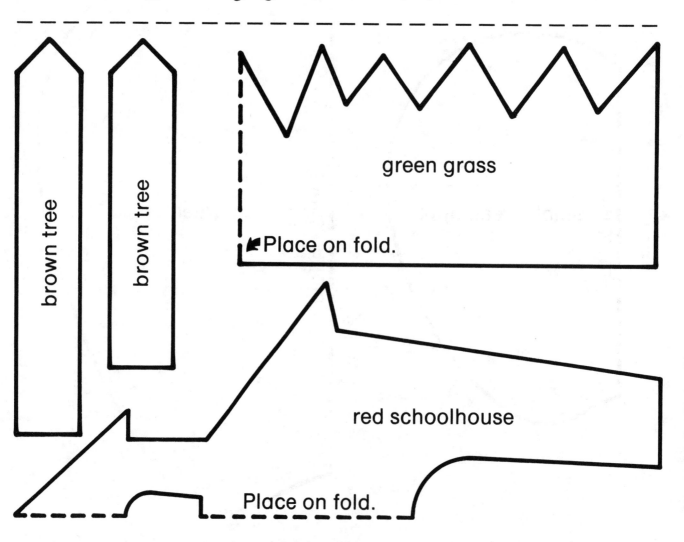

brown tree

brown tree

green grass

◤Place on fold.

red schoolhouse

Place on fold.

Falling Leaves

1. ✏️ around 1 ✋ on brown paper.
2. ✂️ it out.
3. ✂️ out the 〰️🌿▯ below.
4. ✏️ the 〰️ on green paper. ▱
5. ✂️ it out.
6. ✏️ 5 🍂🍂🍂🍂🍂 on orange paper.
7. ✂️ them out.
8. ✏️ the ▯ on brown paper.
9. ✂️ it out.
10. 🖌 the 〰️ 🍂🍂🍂🍂🍂 ▯ ✋ on blue paper.

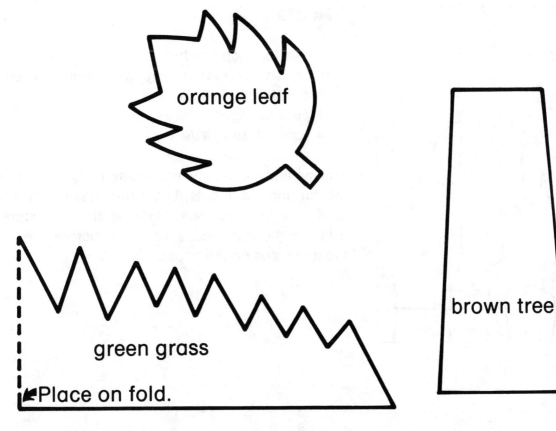

orange leaf

brown tree

green grass

Place on fold.

7

October

Scary Spider

Materials for each child:
- orange and black construction paper
- pattern page
- scissors and paste

Show students how to fold the paper in half and on both diagonals to find the center of the page. The students may use these fold lines as guidelines to begin drawing the spiderweb. Students may work with rulers or other straightedges to mark the spiderweb lines.

Ghosts

Materials for each child:
- brown, black, white, orange, green, and yellow construction paper
- pattern page
- scissors and paste

Tracing and cutting the fence pattern may be challenging for some students, but it provides practice with cutting square corners. Suggest that the students arrange the cut pieces carefully before they glue them in place on the paper.

Jack-o'-Lanterns

Materials for each child:
- orange, green, blue, and black construction paper
- pattern page
- scissors and paste

This page provides practice in tracing and cutting small shapes. Ask students to identify the triangles and half circles. Point out the difference between the triangles used for the eyes and nose of one jack-o'-lantern and the triangle used for the nose of the other jack-o'-lantern.

Hooty Owl

Materials for each child:
- orange, brown, blue, yellow, and black construction paper
- pattern page
- scissors and paste

This art project uses several pattern pieces, and students will have to think about the task as they progress. They should arrange the cut pieces and trim as needed before pasting.

Scary Spider _____

1. around 1 on black paper.

2. it out.

3. ✂ out the ⊚⊚ and the ⑤⑥⑥ below.

4. 🖌 the ⊚⊚ on the 🖐 .

5. ✏ a spider web on orange paper.

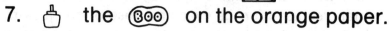

6. 🖌 the 👻 on the ▨ .

7. 🖌 the ⑤⑥⑥ on the orange paper.

- -

eyes

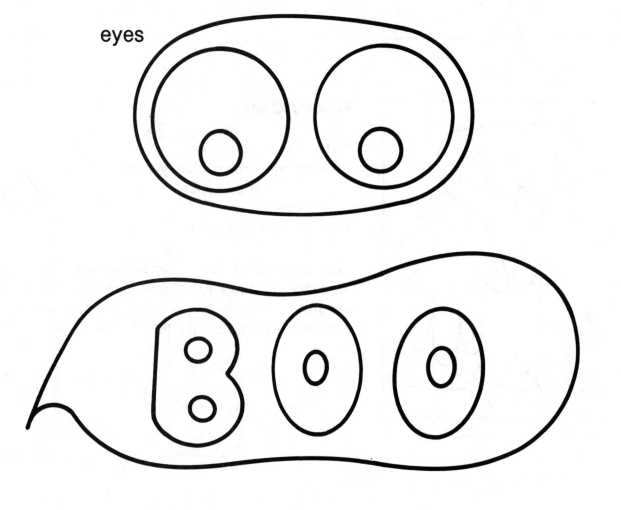

From the Hands of a Child, © 1987

Ghosts _____

1. ✏️ around 2 🖐️ 🖐️ on white paper.
2. ✂️ them out.
3. ✂️ out the ⬭ ▽ ⊞ below.
4. ✏️ the ⊞ on brown paper. ⊞
5. ✂️ it out.
6. ✏️ the ⬭ on orange paper.
7. ✂️ it out.
8. ✏️ the ▽ on green paper.
9. ✂️ it out.
10. ✂️ a corner from a piece of yellow paper. ◻️
11. 🖌️ the ◺ ⬭ ▽ ⊞⊞ 🖐️ 🖐️ on black paper.
12. ✏️ lines on the 🎃 and faces on the 👻 👻 .

- -

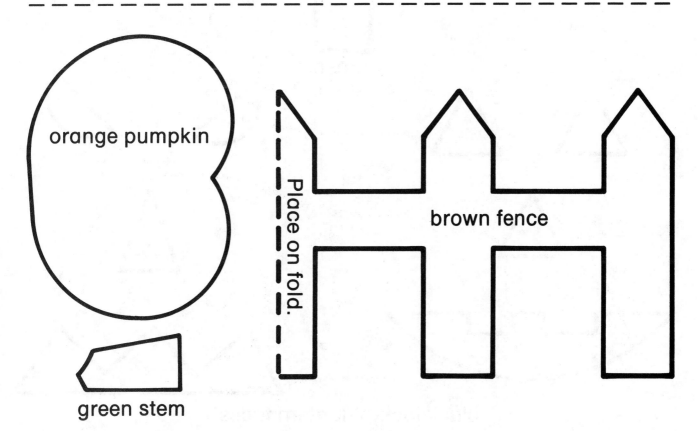

orange pumpkin

green stem

Place on fold.

brown fence

11

Jack-o'-Lanterns _____

1. ✏️ around 2 🖐️ 🖐️ on orange paper.
2. ✂️ them out.
3. ✏️ around 2 🖐️ 🖐️ on green paper.
4. ✂️ them out.
5. ✂️ out the ▯ 🔺🔺 🔺🔺 below.
6. ✏️ the 🔺🔺 🔺🔺 on black paper.
7. ✂️ them out.
8. ✏️ two ▯▯ on green paper.
9. ✂️ them out.
10. 🫙 the 🖐️🖐️🖐️🖐️ 🔺🔺 🔺🔺 ▯▯ on blue paper.

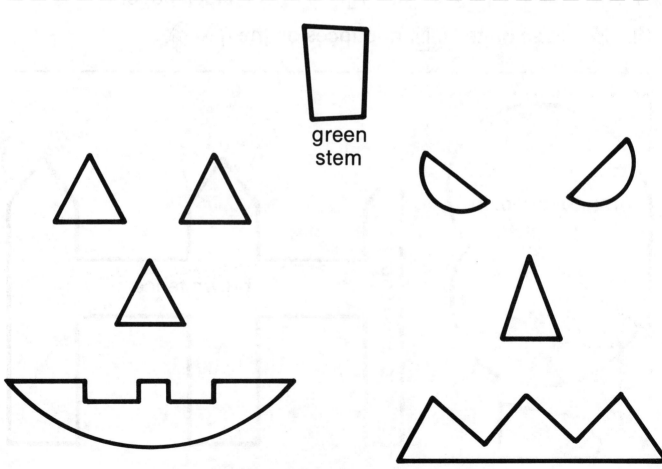

green
stem

black jack-o'-lantern faces

12

Hooty Owl

1. ✏️ around 2 🤚🤚 on orange paper.
2. ✂️ them out.
3. ✂️ out the ○ ♡ ▽ ⌒ ⟋ ⌒ below.
4. ✏️ the ⌒ ⟋ on brown paper.
5. ✂️ them out.
6. ✏️ the ▽ and 2 ⌒ ⌒ on orange paper.
7. ✂️ them out.
8. ✏️ 2 ○ ○ on yellow paper.
9. ✂️ them out.
10. ✏️ 2 ♡ ♡ on black paper.
11. ✂️ them out.
12. 🖌️ the 🤚🤚 ⌒ ◉◉ ▽ ⌒⌒ on blue paper.

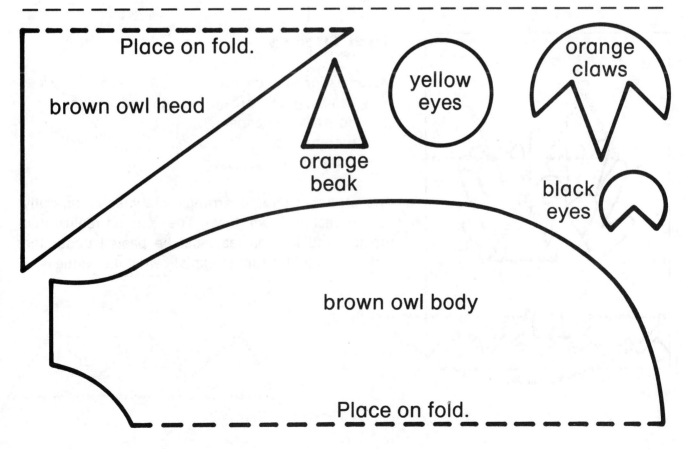

Place on fold.

brown owl head

orange beak

yellow eyes

orange claws

black eyes

brown owl body

Place on fold.

November

Autumn Leaves

Materials for each child:
- brown, yellow, red, and orange construction paper
- pattern page
- scissors and paste
- ruler

Lead a discussion about signs of autumn. Find out how many students have ever helped to rake leaves. See if the students can name some trees that lose their leaves.

This project gives students practice in measuring to the inch. They must find the one-inch and the six-inch marks on the ruler. They must also draw and cut straight edges without a pattern.

Tom Turkey

Materials for each child:
- yellow, green, brown, orange, red, and tan construction paper
- pattern page
- scissors and paste

The students should arrange the pieces carefully before pasting them down. They should realize that the tail and feet pieces must be pasted under the turkey's body. Be sure to explain what the wattle is.

Thanksgiving

Materials for each child:
- white, black, orange, and tan construction paper
- pattern page
- scissors and paste

This project requires some precision cutting to make the pieces match. Show students how to fold the paper and then cut away an interior portion of the pattern (between the woman's arm and body). This is a helpful tip they will use again. Students may, if you wish, attach pieces of yarn for the woman's hair.

Native American

Materials for each child:
- black, orange, white, and blue construction paper
- pattern page
- scissors and paste

This project and the one above are good activities to use when introducing a study lesson on Thanksgiving. Display picture books that show the dress, customs, and life-style of Native Americans in the northeastern part of the United States.

Autumn Leaves

1. ✏️ I 🖐️ on brown paper.
2. ✂️ it out.
3. ✂️ a 1-inch strip of brown paper, 6 inches long. ▯
4. ✂️ out the ◯ 🍁 below.
5. ✏️ 2 ◊◊ on yellow paper.
6. ✂️ them out.
7. ✏️ the 🍁 on orange paper.
8. ✂️ it out.
9. 🧴 the ▮ 🖐️ ◊ 🍁 ◊ on red paper.
10. ✏️ a band across the rake.

orange leaf

yellow leaf

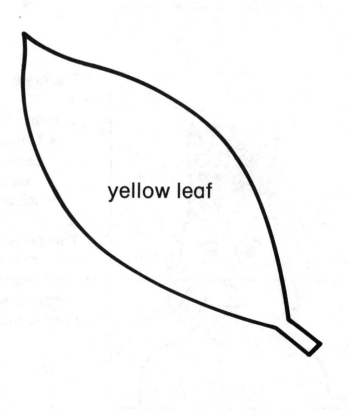

Tom Turkey

1. ✏️ around 1 ✋ on brown paper.

2. ✏️ around 1 ✋ on orange paper.

3. ✏️ around 1 ✋ on red paper.

4. ✂️ them out.

5. ✂️ out the 🦃 〰️ ⚛️ ▽ 〗 below.

6. ✏️ the 🦃 on tan paper. ▱

7. ✂️ it out.

8. ✏️ the ▽ and 2 👣 on orange paper.

9. ✂️ them out.

10. ✏️ the 〰️ on green paper. 📖

11. ✂️ it out.

12. ✏️ the 〗 on red paper.

13. ✂️ it out.

14. 🖊️ the 🥔 👣 👣 〰️ ✋ ✋ ✋ 〗 on yellow paper.

15. ✏️ a face on Tom Turkey.

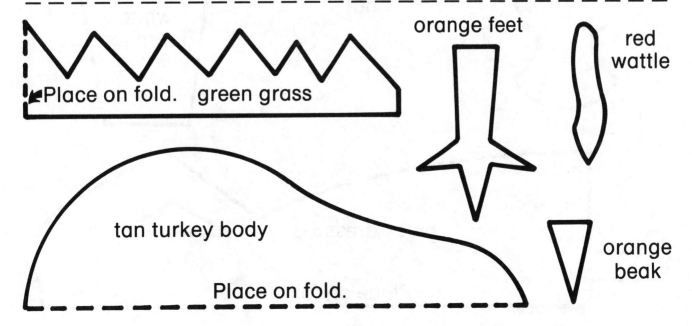

orange feet

red wattle

Place on fold.   green grass

tan turkey body

Place on fold.

orange beak

17

Thanksgiving _____

1. ✏️ around 1 ✋ on white paper.
2. ✂️ it out.
3. ✂️ out the 🌙 Ω ☐ 🚗 below.
4. ✏️ the 🚗 on black paper. 🚗
5. ✂️ it out.
6. ✏️ the Ω on tan paper.
7. ✂️ it out.
8. ✏️ the ☐ 🌙 on white paper.
9. ✂️ them out.
10. 🧴 the 👗 🌙 Ω ☐ ✋ on orange paper.
11. ✏️ a face on the woman.
12. ✏️ hair on the woman.

- -

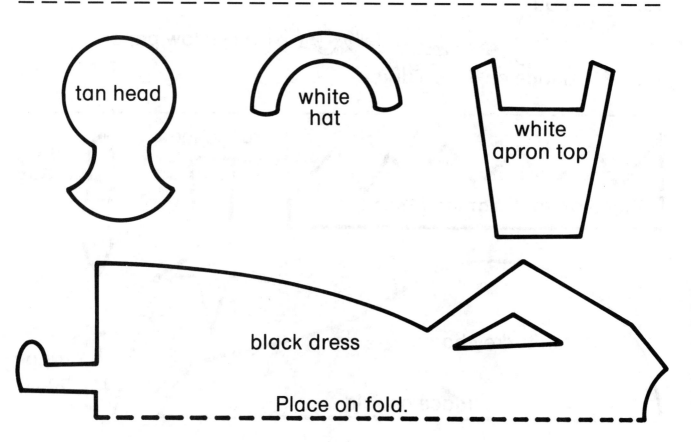

tan head

white hat

white apron top

black dress

Place on fold.

Native American

1. ✏️ around 2 🖐️ 🖐️ on black paper.
2. ✂️ them out.
3. ✂️ out the ⭕ ⬜ 🪶 below.
4. ✏️ the ⭕ ⬜ on orange paper.
5. ✂️ them out.
6. ✏️ the 🪶 on white paper.
7. ✂️ it out.
8. ✏️ the feathers and headband. Use crayons. 🪶
9. 🖌️ the ⬠ ⭕ 🖐️ 🖐️ 🪶 on blue paper.
10. ✏️ a face on the Native American.

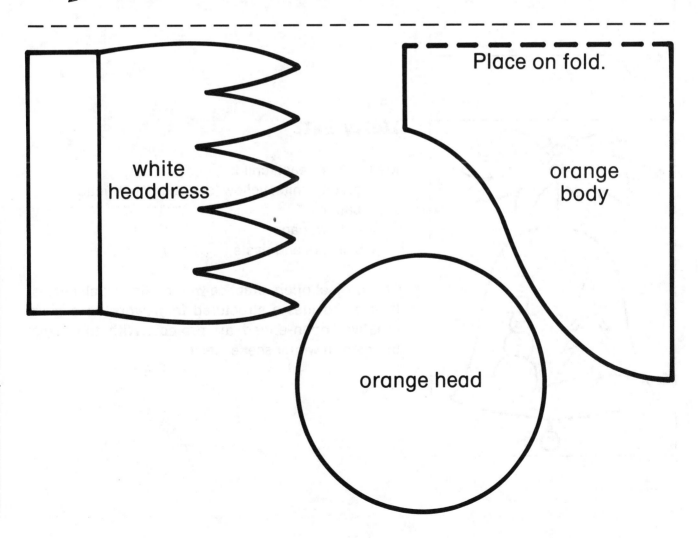

white headdress

Place on fold.

orange body

orange head

December

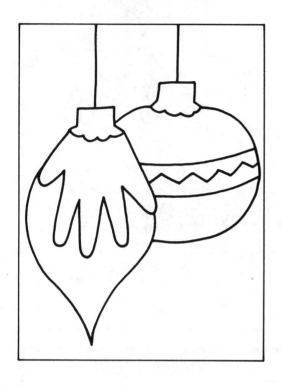

Holiday Ornaments

Materials for each child:
- pink, blue, green, and red construction paper
- pattern page
- scissors and paste

Encourage the students to be creative in drawing designs on the ornaments. As a variation, make a bulletin board display of ornaments; pin up large sheets of green construction paper to form a tree, and help the students pin their ornaments on the tree rather than pasting them on individual sheets of paper.

Holly Bell

Materials for each child:
- green, white, yellow, and red construction paper
- pattern page
- scissors and paste

This project offers practice with cutting small circles. It also provides a structured framework for a more creative, open-ended art project. With the class, brainstorm winter scene ideas.

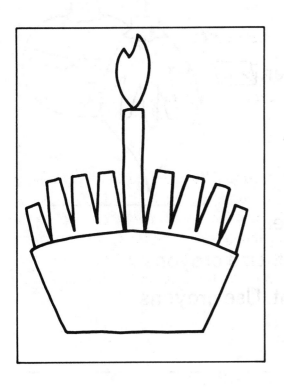

Hanukkah

Materials for each child:
- yellow, brown, purple, and orange construction paper
- pattern page
- scissors and paste

Discuss the meaning of the menorah: there is one candle for each day of the Hanukkah holiday; an additional candle—the *shammash* (meaning "servant")—is used to light the eight candles. The *shammash* is always set apart from the eight candles in some way.

Christmas Angel

Materials for each child:
- white, light blue, dark blue, pink, light brown, dark brown, and yellow construction paper
- pattern page
- scissors and paste

Allow the students to decide the color of the angel's face and hands as well as the color of the hair. Students who choose to give the angel brown skin should, however, use light brown so the drawn facial features will show up.

Holiday Ornaments _____

1. ✏️ around 1 ✋ on red paper.
2. ✂️ it out.
3. ✂️ out the ⌣ ⌢ 𝔸 below.
4. ✏️ the ⌢ and 2 𝔸 on blue paper. ▱
5. ✂️ them out.
6. ✏️ the ⌣ on pink paper. ▱
7. ✂️ it out.
8. 🖊️ the ◊ ✋ ◯ 𝔸 on green paper.
9. ✏️ a pattern on the pink ornament. Use crayons.
10. ✏️ a string to hang each ornament. Use crayons.
11. ✏️ your name on the green paper.

- -

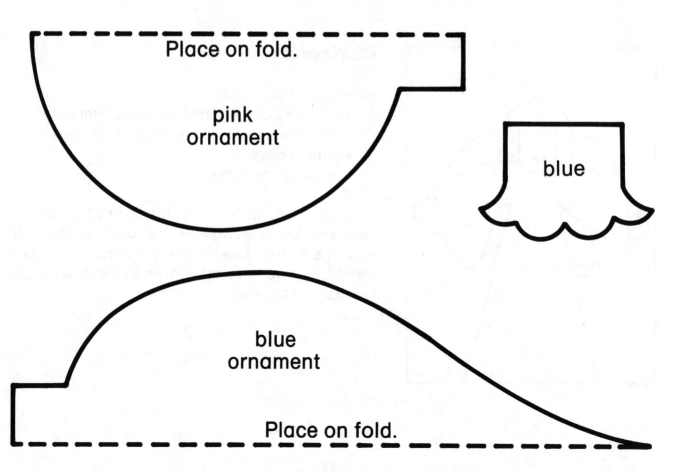

Place on fold.

pink
ornament

blue

blue
ornament

Place on fold.

Holly Bell

1. ✏️ around 2 🖐️ 🖐️ on green paper.

2. ✂️ them out.

3. ✂️ out the ○ 🔔 below.

4. ✏️ the 🔔 on white paper.

5. ✂️ it out.

6. ✏️ 6 ○○○○○○ on red paper.

7. ✂️ them out.

8. 🧴 the 🖐️ 🖐️ 🔔 ⦿⦿⦿ on yellow paper.

9. ✏️ a string to hang the bell.

10. ✏️ a clapper at the bottom of the bell.

11. ✏️ a winter scene on the bell. Use crayons.

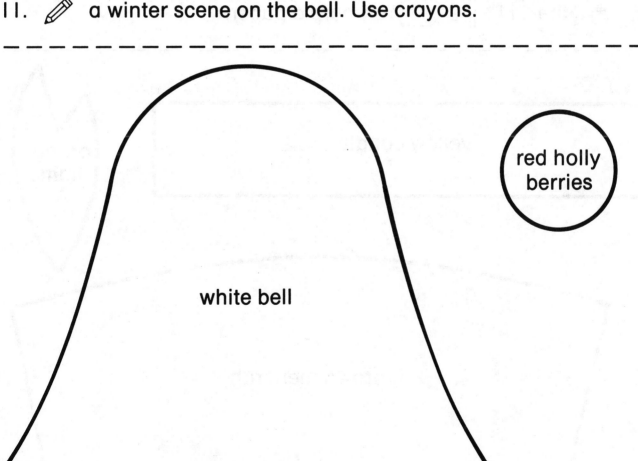

white bell

red holly berries

Hanukkah _____

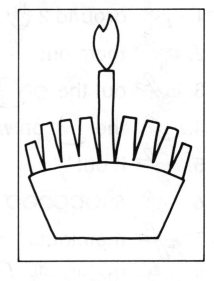

1. ✏️ around 2 🖐️ 🖐️ on yellow paper.
2. ✂️ them out.
3. ✂️ off the ends. 🖐️
4. ✂️ out the ⬯ ▯ ♡ below.
5. ✏️ the ⬯ on brown paper.
6. ✂️ it out.
7. ✏️ the ▯ on yellow paper.
8. ✂️ it out.
9. ✏️ the ♡ on orange paper.
10. ✂️ it out.
11. 🖌️ the 🖐️ 🖐️ ▯ ♡ ⬯ on purple paper.

- -

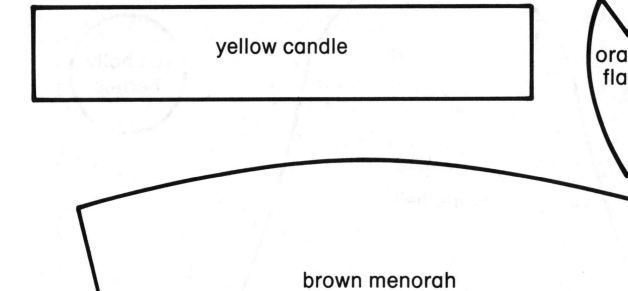

yellow candle

orange flame

brown menorah

Christmas Angel _____

1. ✏️ around 2 🖐️ 🖐️ on white paper.

2. ✂️ them out.

3. ✂️ out the ◿ ⌂ ○ ♡ below.

4. ✏️ the ◿ on light blue paper.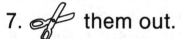

5. ✂️ it out.

6. ✏️ the ○ and 2 ♡♡ on pink or
   light brown paper.

7. ✂️ them out.

8. ✏️ the ⌂ on yellow or dark brown paper.

9. ✂️ it out.

10. 🖊️ the 👕 🖐️ 🖐️ ⌂ ○ 👤 on dark blue paper.

11. ✏️ a face on the angel.

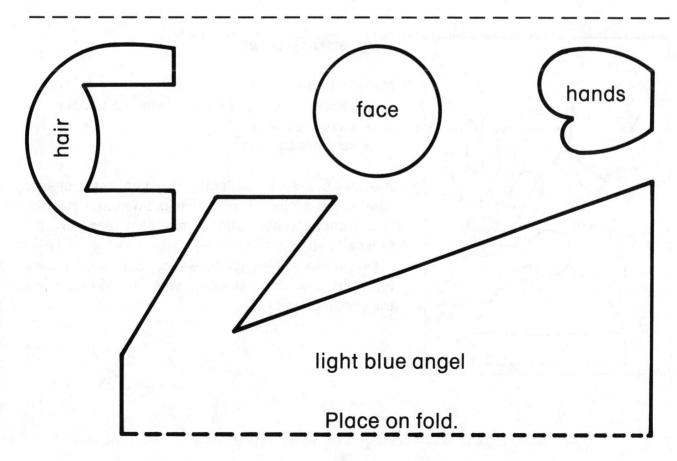

hair

face

hands

light blue angel

Place on fold.

From the Hands of a Child, © 1987

January

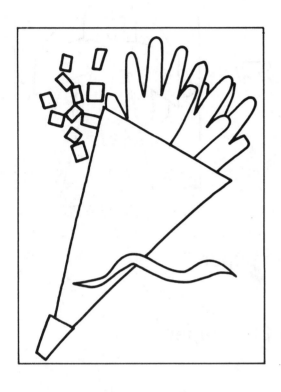

New Year's Noisemaker

Materials for each child:
- orange, pink, yellow, red, and purple construction paper
- pattern page
- scissors and paste

This is a bright and festive art project for a class just leaving for or returning from winter break. The project provides practice with cutting and pasting small pieces of paper in a random pattern.

Cap and Gloves

Materials for each child:
- yellow, green, and blue construction paper
- pattern page
- scissors and paste

Ask the students to identify the two basic shapes used in this project. There are two different rectangles and a circle. (The students may also recognize the finished cap as a half circle.)

Discuss the difference between gloves and mittens. Find out how many students wear knitted caps like the one depicted.

Snowflake

Materials for each child:
- white and purple construction paper
- pattern page
- scissors and paste

This project is a variation of the familiar snowflake-cutting activity; each of the six paper hands is an extended point of the snowflake. Each student should trim off the six paper hands evenly, cutting straight across the hands at the wrists. The students will arrange the six paper hands with the wrist points touching, thus creating a hexagonal space to be covered by the snowflake center pattern.

Frosty Penguin

Materials for each child:
- white, dark blue, black, and orange construction paper
- pattern page
- scissors and paste

This project provides practice with cutting small circles, matching pattern pieces, and cutting neatly. Instruct the students to trace the hand with fingers and thumb together. The penguin stomach piece is placed over the middle three fingers, covering them completely.

New Year's Noisemaker _____

1. ✏️ around 1 🖐️ on yellow paper.

2. ✏️ around 1 🖐️ on red paper.

3. ✏️ around 1 🖐️ on purple paper.

4. ✂️ them out.

5. ✂️ out the ◁▱ ⌐ ∿ below.

6. ✏️ the ◁▱ on orange paper. ▱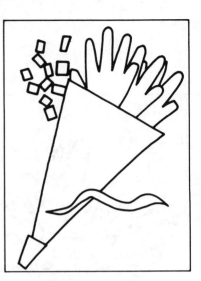

7. ✂️ it out.

8. ✏️ the ⌐ on red paper.

9. ✂️ it out.

10. ✏️ the ∿ on yellow paper.

11. ✂️ it out.

12. 🍶 the 🖐️🖐️🖐️ ◁ ⌐ ∿ on pink paper.

13. ✂️ out tiny squares of paper in any colors.

14. 🍶 them on the pink paper.

- -

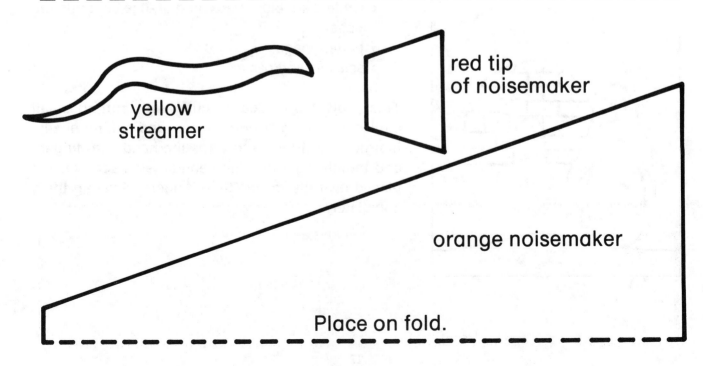

yellow streamer

red tip of noisemaker

orange noisemaker

Place on fold.

From the Hands of a Child, © 1987

Cap and Gloves

1.  around 2 🖐 🖐 on yellow paper.

2. ✂ them out.

3. ✂ out the ▭ ▭ ⌒ ○ below.

4. ✏ the ⌒ on yellow paper.

5. ✂ it out.

6. ✏ the ▭ ○ and 2 ⊟ on

   green paper.

7. ✂ them out.

8. 🖊 the 🖐 🖐 ▭ ⊟ ⌒ ○ on blue paper.

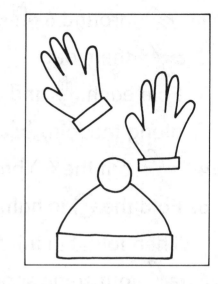

- -

green
pom-pom

green glove bands

yellow
cap

green cap band

Snowflake

1. ✏️ around 6 🖐️🖐️🖐️🖐️🖐️🖐️ on white paper.

2. ✂️ them out.

3. Fold each 🖐️ and ✂️ out 3 ▲▲▲

   along the fold. ⛰️

4. ✂️ out the ⬡ below.

5. Fold the ⬡ in half. ⬭

   Then fold it in thirds. ◁ ▷

6. ✂️ out some shapes along the folds. ▽

7. 🖌️ the 🖐️🖐️🖐️🖐️🖐️⬡ on purple paper.

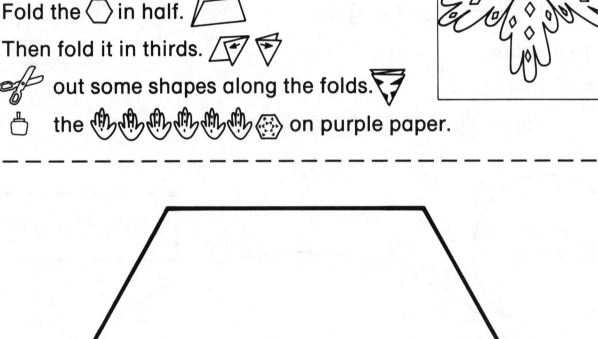

- -

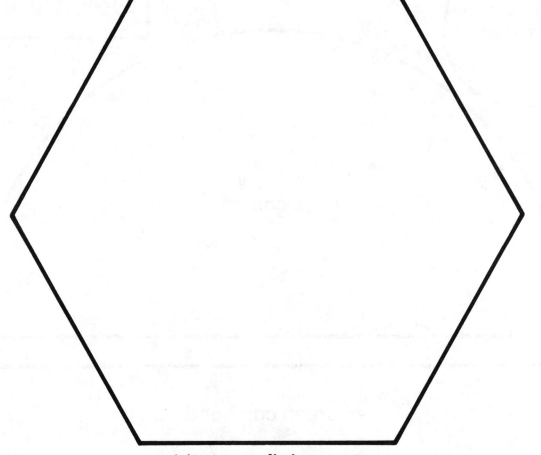

white snowflake center

Frosty Penguin _____

1. ✏️ around 1 ✋ on black paper.

2. ✂️ it out.

3. ✂️ out the ⬭ ⌒ ◯ ◌ below.

4. ✏️ the ⬭ ⌒ ◯ and 2 ∞ on white paper.

5. ✂️ them out.

6. ✏️ the ◗ on orange paper.

7. ✂️ it out.

8. 🧴 the ⬭ ✋ ⌒ ◯ ◌ on blue paper.

9. ✏️ lines on the igloo.

10. ✏️ pupils in the penguin's eyes. ∞

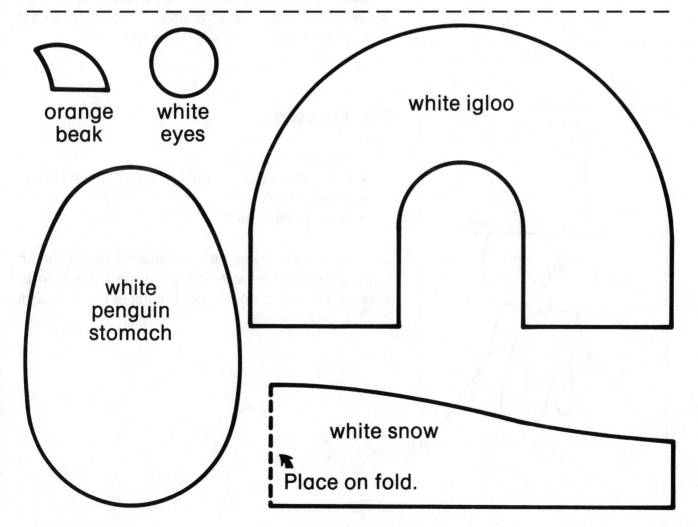

orange
beak

white
eyes

white igloo

white
penguin
stomach

white snow

Place on fold.

February

Valentine

Materials for each child:
- orange, red, white, and pink construction paper
- pattern page
- scissors and paste

This project offers practice cutting scalloped edges; if this is too difficult for the students in your class, have them cut a plain heart shape instead. Remind students to trace a left hand and a right hand. The students should cut the paper hands long, arrange them on the background paper, and then trim them flush with the edge of the background paper.

Encourage the students to be creative with their valentine messages. As a variation, have each student compose a poem to copy onto the heart.

Mr. Lincoln

Materials for each child:
- black, purple, blue, and tan construction paper
- pattern page
- scissors and paste

Introduce a study unit on Abraham Lincoln, or on famous presidents, with this art project. Be sure to show the students how to cut the paper hand to form the top of the beard.

Winter Mountains

Materials for each child:
- white, brown, green, and blue construction paper
- pattern page
- scissors and paste

Students will gain practice cutting points and equal angles. In this art project, they must arrange the pattern pieces to match, but they may also decide where to place some of the pieces to create an attractive picture. As an extension, have the students draw additional trees, animals, cabins, and skiers on the mountains.

Queen of Hearts

Materials for each child:
- orange, yellow, pink, red, and blue construction paper
- pattern page
- scissors and paste

The orange hands make up the Queen's crown, and the yellow hands make up her hair. Students may be able to figure this out, since they cut the bangs from yellow paper. Remind them to arrange pieces before pasting.

Valentine _____

1. ✏️ around 2 🖐️ 🖐️ on orange paper.
2. ✂️ them out.
3. ✂️ out the ⌒⌒ below.
4. ✏️ the ⌒ on red paper. ▱
5. ✂️ it out.
6. ✏️ the ⌒ on white paper. ▱
7. ✂️ it out.
8. ✏️ a message on the heart.
9. 🔖 the ♡ ♡ 🖐️ 🖐️ on pink paper.

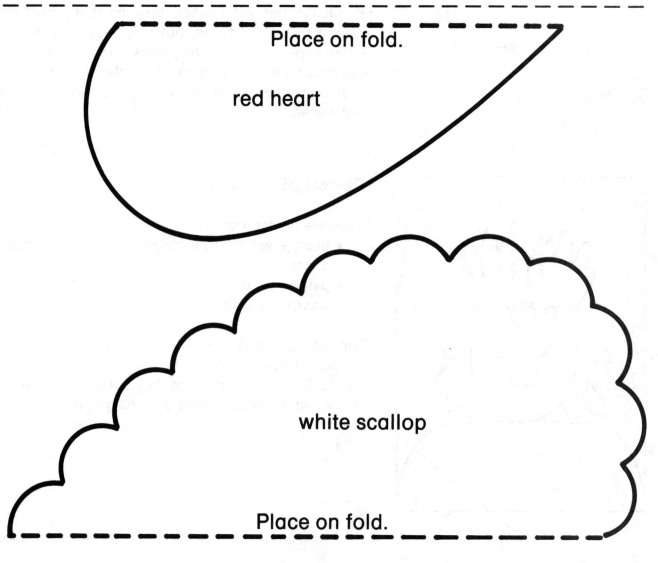

Place on fold.

red heart

white scallop

Place on fold.

From the Hands of a Child, © 1987

Mr. Lincoln

1. ✏️ around 1 ✋ on black paper.
2. ✂️ it out. ✋
3. ✂️ out the 👢 ⅅ ◺ below.
4. ✏️ the ◺ on purple paper. ▱
5. ✂️ it out.
6. ✏️ the 👢 on black paper. ▤
7. ✂️ it out.
8. ✏️ the ⌒ on tan paper. ◠
9. ✂️ it out.
10. 🫙 the △ ○ 🎩 ✋ on blue paper.
11. ✏️ a face on Mr. Lincoln.

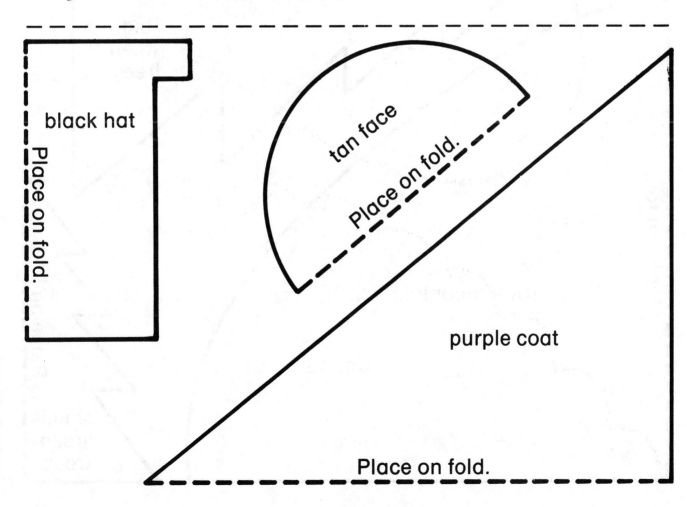

black hat

Place on fold.

tan face

Place on fold.

purple coat

Place on fold.

Winter Mountains

1. ✏️ around 2 🖐️ 🖐️ on white paper.

2. ✂️ them out.

3. ✂️ out the 🔺🌲 below.

4. ✏️ the 🔻 on brown paper. 📄

5. ✂️ it out.

6. ✏️ 1 🌲 and 2 🌲🌲 on green paper. 📄

7. ✂️ them out.

8. 🖌️ the ⬜ 🖐️ 🖐️ 🌲🌲🌲 on blue paper.

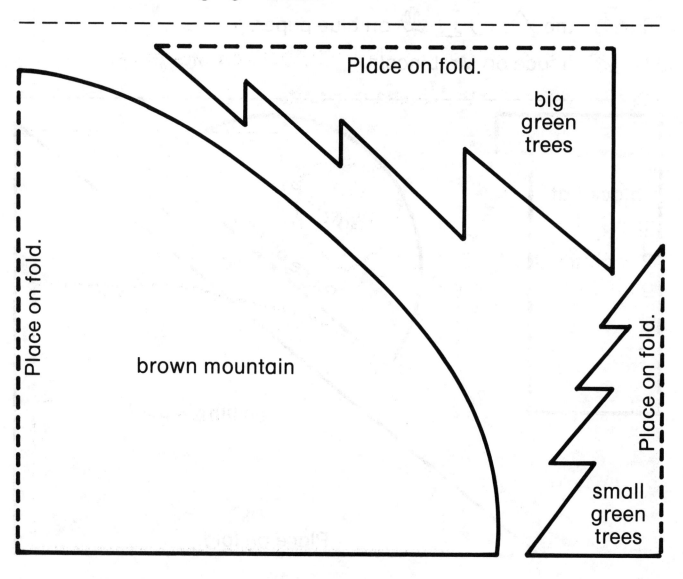

Place on fold.

big green trees

Place on fold.

brown mountain

Place on fold.

small green trees

Queen of Hearts

1. ✏️ around 2 🖐️🖐️ on orange paper.

2. ✏️ around 2 🖐️🖐️ on yellow paper.

3. ✂️ them out.

4. ✂️ out the ◖ ♡ ◗ below.

5. ✏️ the ◖ on orange paper.

6. ✂️ it out.

7. ✏️ the ◗ on pink paper.

8. ✂️ it out.

9. ✏️ 5 ♡♡♡♡♡ on red paper.

10. ✂️ them out.

11. 🧴 the ⬤ ◯ 🖐️ 🖐️ 🖐️ 🖐️ ♡♡♡♡♡ on blue paper.

12. ✏️ a face on the Queen of Hearts.

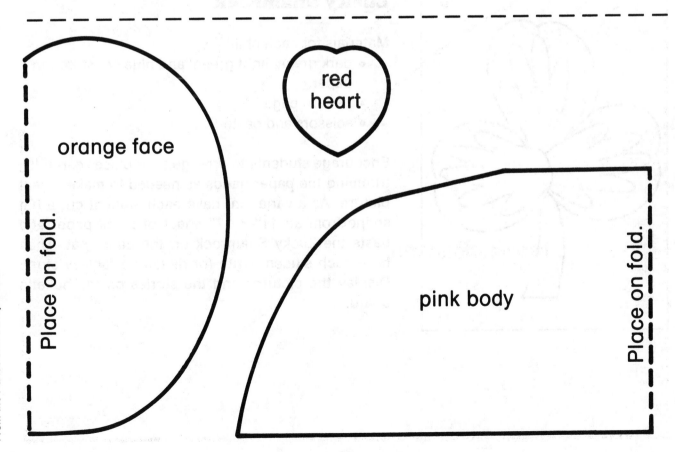

red heart

orange face

Place on fold.

pink body

Place on fold.

March

Spring Flowers

Materials for each child:
- green, brown, red, and yellow construction paper
- pattern page
- scissors and paste

Use this project to reinforce the difference between long and short and between small and big. Discuss what type of flowers have been depicted; if students trace their hands in a tight position, the flower will resemble a tulip. Encourage students to draw detail on the leaves of the flowers.

Lucky Shamrock

Materials for each child:
- dark green, light green, and blue construction paper
- pattern page
- scissors and paste

Encourage students to arrange their pieces carefully, trimming the paper hands as needed to make a neat picture. As a variation, have each student cut a hat shape from an 11" × 17" sheet of black paper and paste the Lucky Shamrock on the paper hat. Then have each student write (or dictate) a fantasy story. Display the pictures and the stories on the bulletin board.

Butterfly

Materials for each child:
- yellow, orange, and green construction paper
- pattern page
- scissors and paste

Ask students to identify the shape of the butterfly spots. The spots are ovals. Have the students compare the ovals with circles.

As a variation, have students cut out four paper hands and paste two on each side of the butterfly's body. This will create a more realistic butterfly. The students may also draw abstract designs on the butterfly wings instead of pasting spots.

Taking Flight

Material for each child:
- brown, tan, and blue construction paper
- pattern page
- scissors and paste

Make sure students understand they must tuck one paper hand under the bird's body. Although this project is simple, the students must match the end of the tail section to the bird's body and paste them neatly together.

Butterfly _____

1. ✏️ around 2 🖐🖐 on yellow paper.
2. ✂️ them out.
3. ✂️ out the 🧴○ below.
4. ✏️ the 🧴 and 4 ⚌ on orange paper.
5. ✂️ them out.
6. 🧴 the 🧴 🖐🖐 ⚌ on green paper.
7. ✏️ eyes on the butterfly.

- -

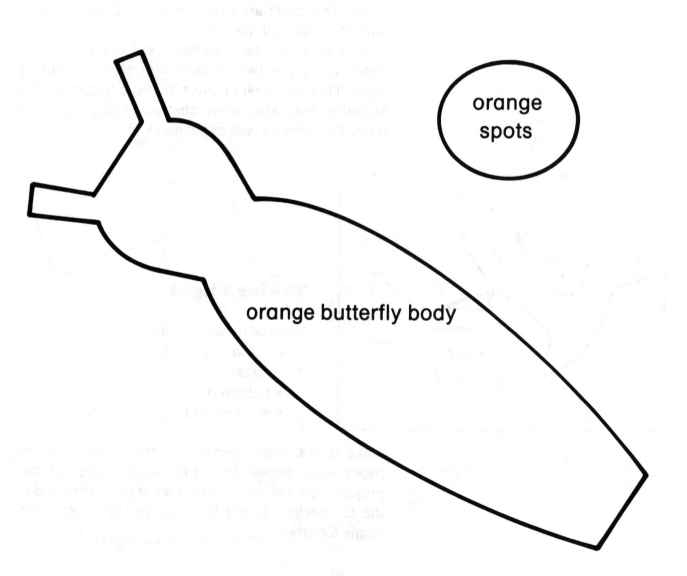

orange spots

orange butterfly body

From the Hands of a Child, © 1987

Taking Flight

1. ✏️ around 2 🖐️🖐️ on brown paper.

2. ✂️ them out.

3. ✂️ out the 🐦◁ below.

4. ✏️ the ◁ on brown paper.

5. ✂️ it out.

6. ✏️ the 🐦 on tan paper.

7. ✂️ it out.

8. ✏️ the 🐦 🖐️ 🖐️ ◁ on blue paper.

9. ✏️ an eye on the bird.

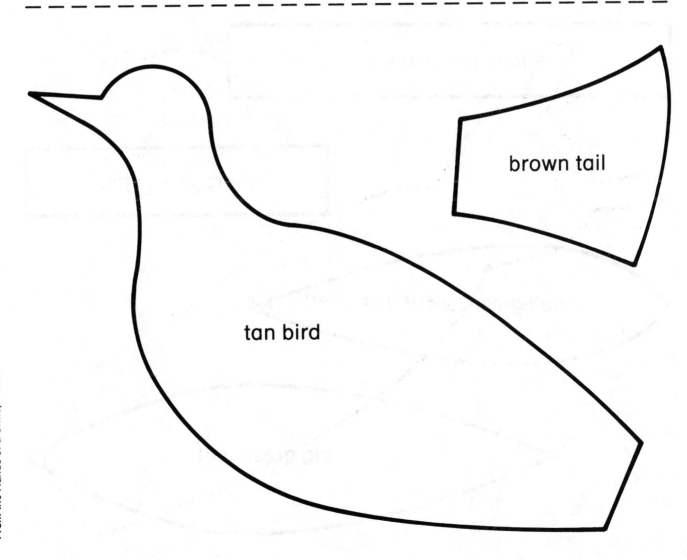

brown tail

tan bird

Spring Flowers

1. ✏️ around 1 ✋ on yellow paper.

2. ✏️ around 1 ✋ on red paper.

3. ✂️ them out.

4. ✂️ out the ▭ ◯ below.

5. ✏️ the ▭ , the ▭ , 2 ◯ , and

   2 ◯ on green paper.

6. ✂️ them out.

7. 🖌️ the ▯▯◯◯◯◯ ✋ ✋ on brown paper.

- -

long green stem

short green stem

small green leaf

big green leaf

42

Lucky Shamrock

1. ✏️ around 3 🖐️🖐️🖐️ on dark green paper.

2. ✂️ them out.

3. ✂️ out the ⬭∖ below.

4. ✏️ 3 ⬭⬭⬭ on light green paper.

5. ✂️ them out.

6. ✏️ the ∖ on dark green paper.

7. ✂️ it out.

8. 🖌️ the ⬭⬭⬭ 🖐️🖐️🖐️ ∖ on blue paper.

- -

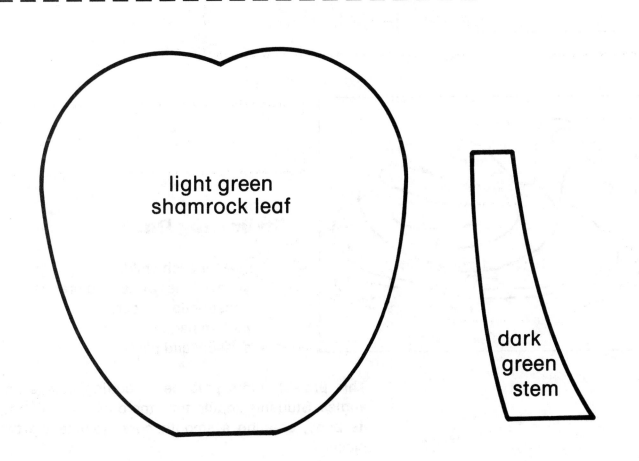

light green
shamrock leaf

dark
green
stem

April

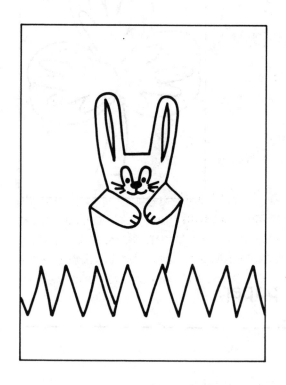

Springtime Bunny

Materials for each child:
- green, blue, and white construction paper
- pattern page
- scissors and paste

This project challenges students' ability to follow written and pictorial directions. You may wish to model the paper hand cutting and folding so that students will be able to understand the directions more easily. Make sure that students trace their hands in a spread position.

Swimming Duck

Materials for each child:
- yellow, blue, white, and orange construction paper
- pattern page
- scissors and paste

This project offers practice in cutting curves and angles. Students should tuck the duck's head under its body, creating a smooth curve joining the two pieces.

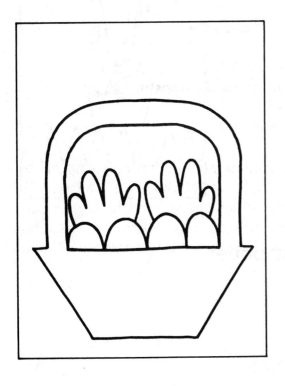

Basket of Eggs

Materials for each child:
- green, brown, blue, white, and tan construction paper
- pattern page
- scissors and paste

In this project, the paper hands represent grass inside the basket. Capable students may wish to draw lines on the basket, showing the pattern of woven reeds. If your class celebrates Easter, have the students draw abstract designs on the eggs, using crayons or felt-tipped markers in bright colors.

Cheery Chick

Materials for each child:
- white, yellow, orange, and green construction paper
- pattern page
- scissors and paste

After the students have completed their pictures, have them name words that begin with the consonant blend *ch.* Each student will then list several *ch* words on Cheery Chick's body.

Springtime Bunny

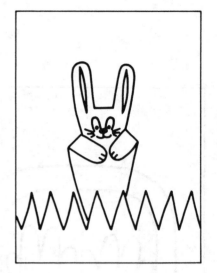

1. ✏️ around 1 ✋ on white paper.
2. ✂️ it out.
3. Fold the middle finger under. ✋
4. Fold down the thumb and the pinky finger. ✌️
5. ✂️ out the 〰️ below.
6. ✏️ the 〰️ on green paper. 🗂️
7. ✂️ it out.
8. 🖌️ the ✌️ and the 〰️ on blue paper.
9. ✏️ a face on the bunny.
10. ✏️ paws on the bunny.
11. ✏️ the inside of the bunny's ears pink.

- -

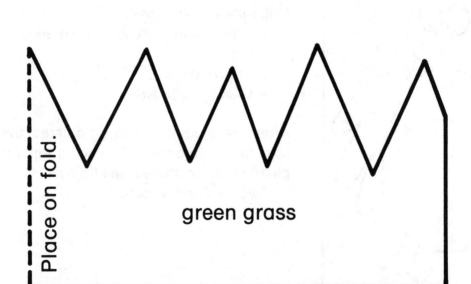

Place on fold.

green grass

Swimming Duck

1. ✏️ around 1 🖐️ on white paper.
2. ✂️ it out.
3. ✂️ out the 🪶 𝑞 ⟩ 🦶 below.
4. ✏️ the 🪶 𝑞 on yellow paper.
5. ✂️ them out.
6. ✏️ the ⟩ and 2 🦶🦶 on orange paper.
7. ✂️ them out.
8. 🗜️ the 🪶 𝑞 🖐️ 🦶🦶 ⟩ on blue paper.
9. ✏️ an eye on the duck.
10. ✏️ water lines around the duck.

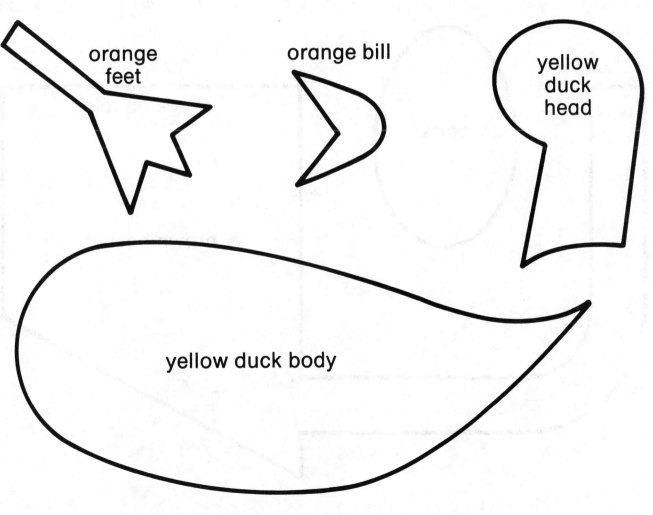

orange feet

orange bill

yellow duck head

yellow duck body

Basket of Eggs _____

1. ✏️ around 2 ✋✋ on green paper.
2. ✂️ them out.
3. ✂️ out the ✋O below.
4. ✏️ the ✋ on brown paper.
5. ✂️ it out.
6. ✏️ 2 O on white paper.
7. ✂️ them out.
8. ✏️ 2 O on tan paper.
9. ✂️ them out.
10. 🧴 the ✋✋ 🧺 OO OO on blue paper.

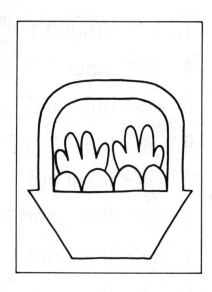

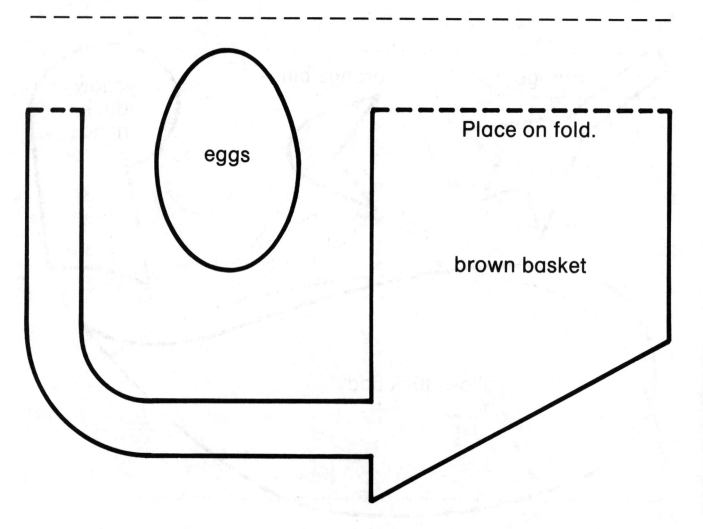

eggs

Place on fold.

brown basket

From the Hands of a Child, © 1987

Cheery Chick _____

1. ✏️ around 2 🖐️🖐️ on white paper.

2. ✂️ them out.

3. ✂️ out the ⟆ ⟅ 🦶 ο ▽ below.

4. ✏️ the ⟆ ⌒ on yellow paper. ▱

5. ✂️ them out.

6. ✏️ the ▽ and 2 🦶🦶 on orange paper.

7. ✂️ them out.

8. ✏️ 2 ◯◯ on white paper.

9. ✂️ them out.

10. 🗴 the ◯ ο 🖐️ 🖐️ 🦶🦶 οο ▽ on green paper.

11. ✏️ pupils in the chick's eyes. ◖◗

- -

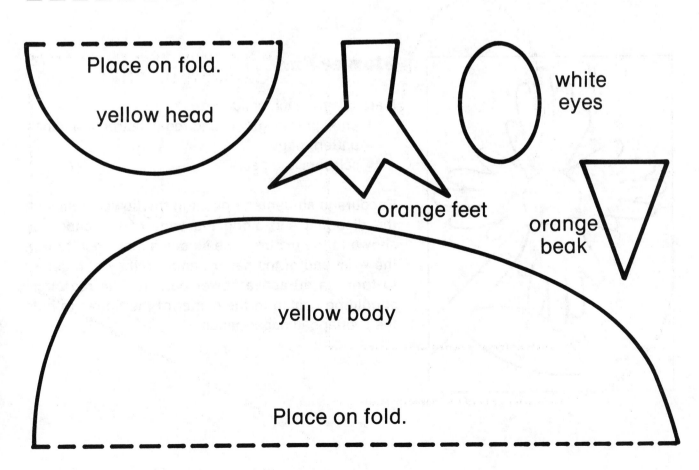

Place on fold.

yellow head

orange feet

white eyes

orange beak

yellow body

Place on fold.

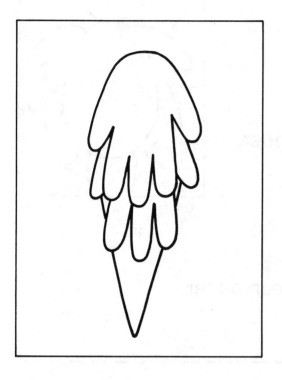

Ice-Cream Cone

Materials for each child:
- blue, white, pink, and brown construction paper
- pattern page
- scissors and paste

This project is very easy for most primary students. Students who need a challenge may draw crisscross lines on the cone, using a black crayon or felt-tipped marker. Encourage the students to choose different colors for the scoops of ice cream or to draw bits (raisins, fruit, nuts, or chocolate chips) in the ice cream.

Flower Fun

Materials for each child:
- pink, purple, green, and red construction paper
- pattern page
- scissors and paste

Encourage students to position the flower stem with the diagonal end along the edge of the paper, as shown in the picture. The students may need to trim the wrist end of the paper hands so they fit together to form an attractive flower pattern. The red circle should be pasted in the center of the flower to hide the overlapped paper hands.

May Basket

Materials for each child:
- brown, green, orange, pink, and yellow construction paper
- pattern page
- scissors and paste

In this project, the paper hands form the basket. They should be trimmed so they do not extend beneath the base of the basket. Ask students to identify the two basic shapes—circle and rectangle—in this project.

Clowning Around

Materials for each child:
- pink, red, white, and blue construction paper
- pattern page
- scissors and paste

This project may be challenging for some students. Make sure the students understand that the two red paper hands create the clown's hair, and the three pink paper hands create the clown's collar. There are three basic shapes—triangle, circles (small and big), and rectangle—in this project for the students to identify.

Ice-Cream Cone

1. ✏️ around 1 🖐️ on white paper.
2. ✏️ around 1 ✋ on pink paper.
3. ✂️ them out.
4. ✂️ out the ◁ below.
5. ✏️ the ◁ on brown paper.
6. ✂️ it out.
7. 🔖 the ◁ 🖐️ ✋ on blue paper.

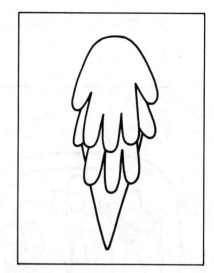

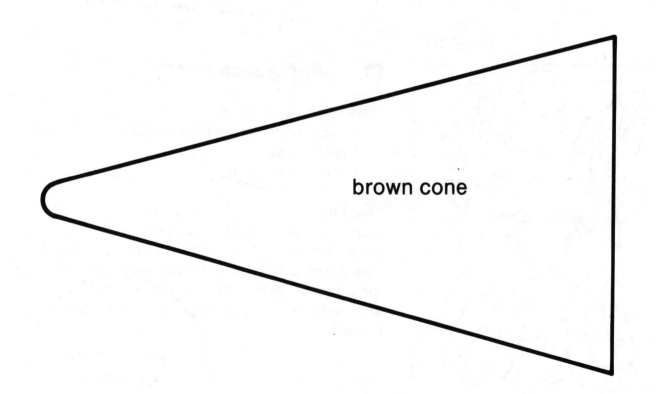

brown cone

From the Hands of a Child, © 1987

Flower Fun

1. ✏️ around 4 🖐️ 🖐️ 🖐️ 🖐️ on pink paper.
2. ✂️ them out.
3. ✂️ out the ◇ ⬭ ○ below.
4. ✏️ the ◇ ⬭ on green paper.
5. ✂️ them out.
6. ✏️ the ○ on red paper.
7. ✂️ it out.
8. 🖌️ the 🖐️ 🖐️ 🖐️ 🖐️ | ◇ ○ on purple paper.

- -

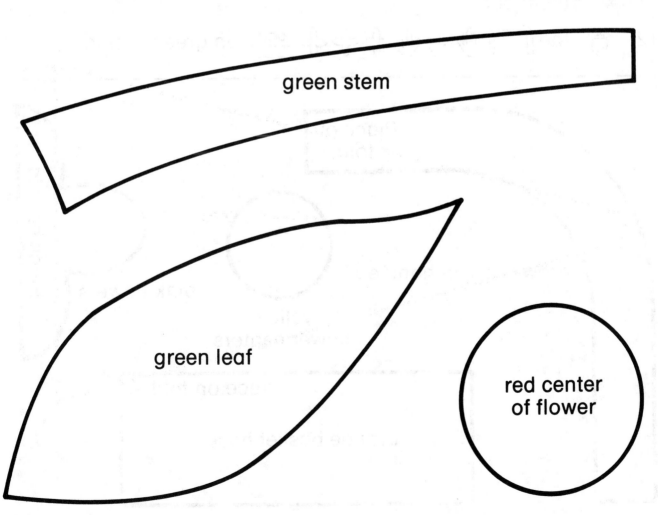

green stem

green leaf

red center
of flower

May Basket

1. ✏️ around 3 🖐️🖐️🖐️ on brown paper.
2. ✂️ them out.
3. ✂️ out the ⌐ ▭ ⊰ ○ below.
4. ✏️ the ⌐ on brown paper. 📄
5. ✂️ it out.
6. ✏️ the ▭ on orange paper. 📄
7. ✂️ it out.
8. ✏️ 3 ⊰⊰⊰ on pink paper. 📄
9. ✂️ them out.
10. ✏️ 3 ∘∘∘ on yellow paper.
11. ✂️ them out.
12. 🖌️ the ⌒ 🖐️🖐️🖐️ ✛✛✛ ▭ on green paper.

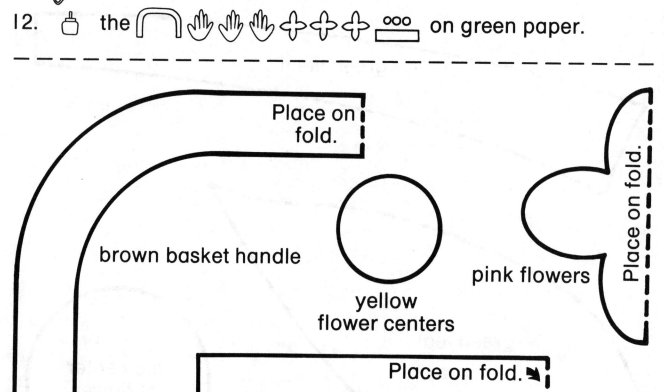

Place on fold.

brown basket handle

yellow flower centers

pink flowers

Place on fold.

Place on fold. ◥

orange basket base

Clowning Around _____

1. ✏️ around 5 🖐️🖐️🖐️🖐️🖐️ on pink paper (collar and hair).

2. ✂️ them out.

3. ✂️ out the ⌣ ◗▯ ⚇ ◺ below.

4. ✏️ the ◗ ◺ ⚇ on red paper. ◿

5. ✂️ them out.

6. ✏️ the ▯ ○ on pink paper. ▥

7. ✂️ them out.

8. ✏️ the ⌣ on white paper. ⏢

9. ✂️ it out.

10. 🧴 the ⌒ 🖐️🖐️🖐️🖐️🖐️ ○ ▲ ⚇ on blue paper.

11. ✏️ 2 eyes and mouth line.

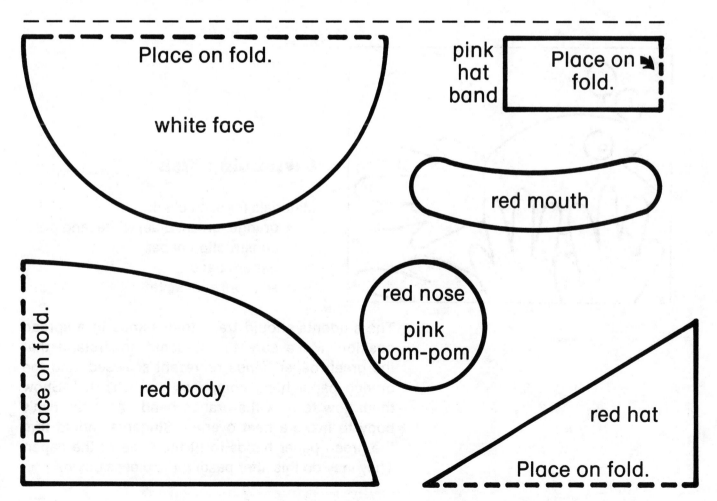

Place on fold.

white face

pink hat band   Place on ↘ fold.

red mouth

red body

Place on fold.

red nose

pink pom-pom

red hat

Place on fold.

June

Summer Sun

Materials for each child:
- yellow, orange, blue, white, and black construction paper
- pattern page
- scissors and paste

This project is very easy for most primary students. Encourage them to use their imaginations as they draw faces on their suns. Use the basic shapes in this project to show the difference between ovals and circles.

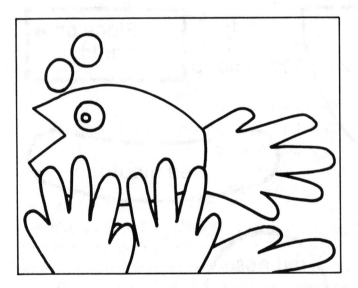

Swimming Fish

Materials for each child:
- orange, green, blue, white, and gray construction paper
- pattern page
- scissors and paste

The students should trace their hands in a spread position. Make sure the students understand that the green paper hands represent seaweed, and the orange paper hand comprises the fish's tail. Show them how to tuck the orange hand under the fish's body to make a neat overlap. Students should trim the green paper hands to fit the edge of the paper. They may do this after pasting the pieces down.

Sailing Time

Materials for each child:
- light blue, dark blue, white, yellow, and brown construction paper
- pattern page
- scissors and paste
- ruler

Ask the students to compare the two sails and tell which is small and which is big. Ask them to identify the shape of each sail. Some students may think that the boat is a rectangle; explain that it is not a rectangle, even though it has four sides, and draw a real rectangle on the chalkboard.

This project requires students to measure with a ruler, finding inch and ½-inch increments. It also gives students an opportunity to draw and cut straight lines without a pattern.

Baseball Player

Materials for each child:
- black, blue, pink, brown, white, and red construction paper
- pattern page
- scissors and paste

Cutting the cap may be difficult for some children. They must carefully paste the cap and visor, matching the edges, and must make sure the paper hands (the player's hair) are tucked under the cap. Encourage students to give their baseball players some personality.

Summer Sun

1. ✏️ around 4 🖐️ 🖐️ 🖐️ 🖐️ on yellow paper.
2. ✂️ them out.
3. ✂️ out the ⌓ ◯ ○ below.
4. ✏️ the ⌓ on orange paper.
5. ✂️ it out.
6. ✏️ 2 ◯ ○ on white paper.
7. ✂️ them out.
8. ✏️ 2 ◯ ○ on black paper.
9. ✂️ them out.
10. 🧴 the 🖐️ 🖐️ 🖐️ 🖐️ ◯ ○ ◯ on blue paper.
11. ✏️ a nose and mouth on the sun.

- -

white eyes

black pupils

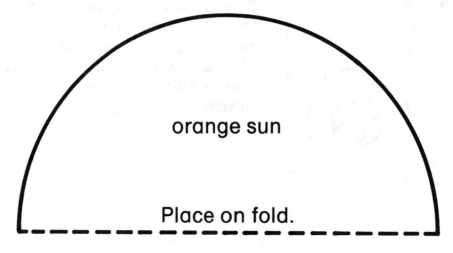

orange sun

Place on fold.

From the Hands of a Child, © 1987

Swimming Fish _____

1. ✏️ around 1 🖐️ on orange paper (fish tail).

2. ✏️ around 3 🖐️ 🖐️ 🖐️ on green paper (seaweed).

3. ✂️ them out.

4. ✂️ out the ⬭ ○ ○ below.

5. ✏️ the ⬭ on orange paper.

6. ✂️ it out.

7. ✏️ the ○ on white paper.

8. ✏️ 2 ○ ○ on gray paper.

9. ✂️ them out.

10. 🫙 the ⬭ 🖐️ ° ° 🖐️ 🖐️ 🖐️ on blue paper.

11. ✏️ a pupil on the fish's eye.

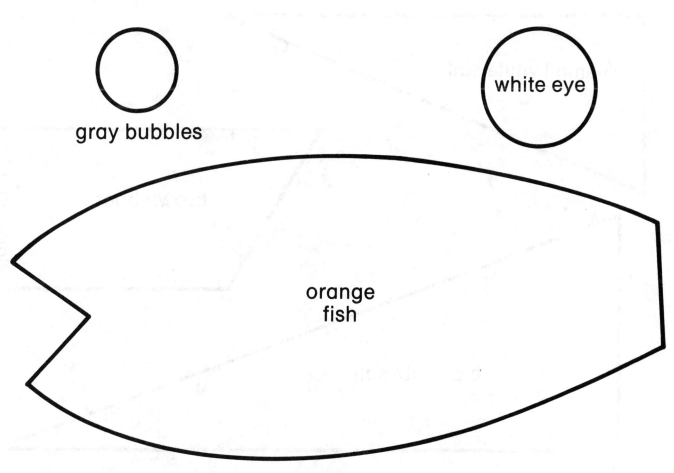

gray bubbles

white eye

orange
fish

Sailing Time

1. ✏️ around 2 🖐️🖐️ on light blue paper.
2. ✏️ around 2 🖐️🖐️ on dark blue paper.
3. ✏️ around 2 🖐️🖐️ on white paper.
4. ✂️ them out.
5. ✂️ out the ◺◹ ⬯ below.
6. ✏️ the ◺◹ on white paper.
7. ✂️ them out.
8. ✏️ the ⬯ on brown paper.
9. ✂️ it out.
10. ✂️ a ½-inch strip of brown paper, 7 inches long.
11. 🖊️ the ⬯ | ◺◹ 🖐️🖐️🖐️🖐️🖐️🖐️ on yellow paper.

- -

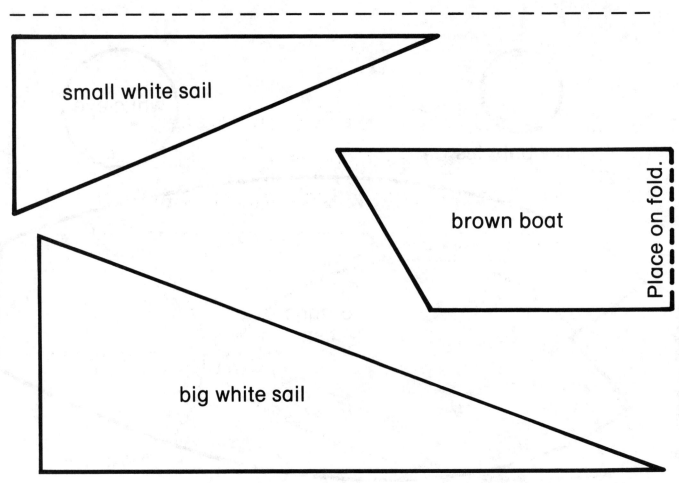

small white sail

brown boat

Place on fold.

big white sail

From the Hands of a Child, © 1987

Baseball Player _____

1. ✏️ around 2 ✋✋ on black paper.

2. ✂️ them out.

3. ✂️ out the ⬭ ◯ below,

   and the ▱ ♡ ◯ ❨ on the next page.

4. ✏️ the ◯ on pink or brown paper.

5. ✂️ it out.

6. ✏️ the ⬭ ▱ on blue paper. 📄

7. ✂️ them out.

8. ✏️ the ⌣ on black paper.

9. ✂️ it out.

10. ✏️ the ♡ on brown paper.

11. ✂️ it out.

12. ✏️ the ◯ on white paper.

13. ✂️ it out.

14. 🖊️ the ⬭ ✋ ✋ ◯ ⬭ ♡ ◯ on red paper.

15. ✏️ a face on the baseball player.

16. ✏️ lines on the hat and the ball 🧢 ⚾ and the shirt.

From the Hands of a Child, © 1987 David S. Lake Publishers

- -

blue cap

white baseball

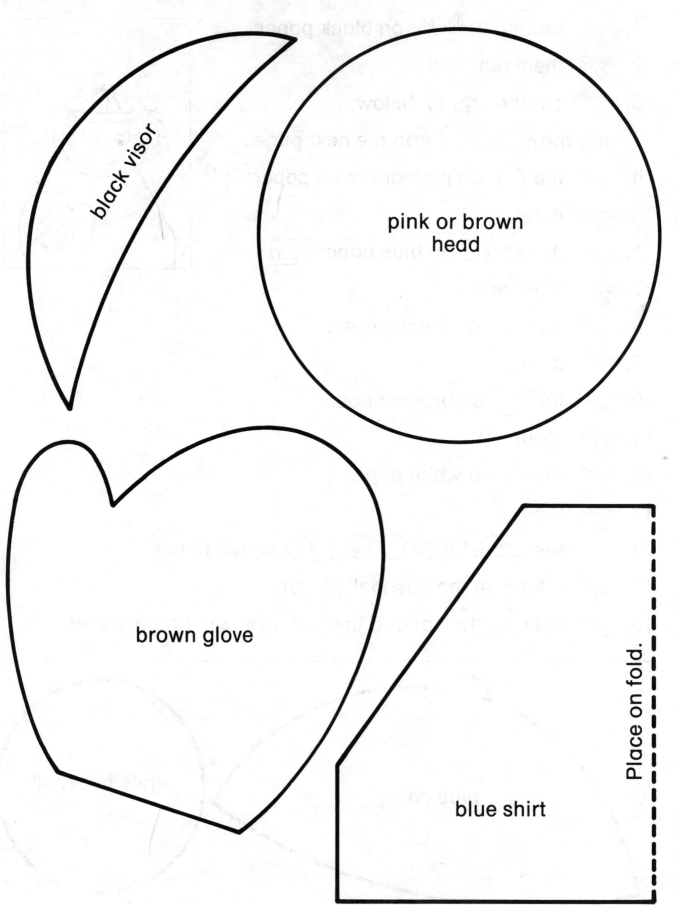

black visor

pink or brown
head

brown glove

blue shirt

Place on fold.